How to Overcome Sexual Abuse

Nat Greg

How to Overcome Sexual Abuse

INTRODUCTION

Assaults of a sexual nature can take a variety of different forms. On the other hand, the emotional toll that smoking takes on your life is frequently consistent.

After suffering an assault, it is possible to move on in a way that is beneficial to one's health. You can get through this by learning and putting into practice healthy coping skills, which can help you get through it so you can move on with your life and live it to the fullest in the future.

The following are some examples of sexual assault:

- A failed attempt to commit rape
- Sexual touching that isn't requested, like fondling
- Forcing a victim to engage in sexual activity, such as oral sex, against their will.
- The act of penetrating the victim's body is defined as rape.

The term "physical force" does not always refer to "force." Some abusers resort to psychological tactics such as pressure or manipulation in order to force their victims to engage in sexual activity against their will. They might also resort to intimidating techniques or threatening language.

According to the Centers for Disease Control and Prevention (CDC), one in three women and one in four men will, at some point in their lives, be the victims of sexual assault that involves the use of physical contact.

However, a significant number of these people never seek treatment of any kind. A few of them have the impression that their assault was "too trivial" to warrant much attention or that it took place "too many years ago." Others feel too humiliated or ashamed to tell anyone else what is going on. And there are those people who don't believe they require assistance or don't even know how to get it if they do.

The incidence of sexual trauma is, however, far from an isolated problem. Recent statistics from throughout the world demonstrate that one in three women have been the victims of physical and/or sexual assault at the hands of a relationship or of sexual violence at the hands of a person other than a partner. (The vast majority of these assaults are committed by intimate partners, which means that the abusers are not total strangers.) Around twenty percent of the world's female population has come forward to say that they were sexually abused as children. And the fact that sexual assault is all too widespread on American college campuses is no longer a well-kept secret in the United States. In a 2015 poll conducted by the Association of American Universities at a total of twenty-seven universities, including seven members of the prestigious Ivy League, more than 20% of female students reported having had sexual contact without their consent.

There are many different ways to find recovery, despite the fact that this information is utterly depressing (even if you haven't personally suffered sexual trauma, it's highly probable that you know someone who has). We had a conversation with Dr. Lori Brotto, a psychologist who is a professor in the Department of Obstetrics and Gynecology at the University of British Columbia. Dr. Brotto is also the director of the UBC Sexual Health Laboratory, where she treats patients who are experiencing a variety of sexual difficulties. Unfortunately, but not unexpectedly, a significant number of Dr. Brotto's patients have suffered some form of sexual abuse. It is not your fault. We are immensely resilient by nature, and it is never too late to resolve an issue around sexual trauma. Below, she outlines the healing process and emphasizes these major lessons.

For many people who have survived sexual assault, traumatic events can be triggered by high-profile instances like the one involving Bill Cosby. Having a solid support system might be helpful when you're going through a difficult time.

According to the CDC, more than one in three women and one in four men will suffer sexual violence at some point in their lifetime.

An overturned conviction for aggravated indecent assault against the disgraced entertainer Bill Cosby and his sudden release from prison has undoubtedly been a trigger for many survivors of sexual assault. This means that it has brought about distressing memories of their own experience or a strong emotional or physiological reaction in them.

According to Elizabeth L. Jeglic, PhD, a professor of psychology at the John Jay College of Criminal Justice at the City University of New York, the decision of the court has resulted in a "tremendous outcry" from advocacy groups that support survivors. This is because of the reason stated in the previous sentence.

According to Dr. Jeglic, "Sexual abuse is the most underreported crime, and it is believed that only around one-third of survivors (37 percent) report the crime to the authorities." "What is even more frustrating is the fact that just 25 out of every 1,000 cases of sexual assault result in the perpetrator being sentenced to jail,"

The Centers for Disease Control and Prevention (CDC) reports that sexual violence, which is defined as any form of sexual contact that takes place without the recipient's consent, is extremely prevalent. More than one in three women and one in four men will experience sexual violence at some point in their lives. Jeglic says that people who have been sexually assaulted may not want to report it because they have a bad opinion of the criminal justice system and know that convictions in these cases are very rare.

Shauna Springer, PhD, a trauma expert based in California and the chief psychologist at the Stella Center, notes that when a high-profile sexual assault case unfolds in court, it can cause different reactions among survivors of sexual assault. Shauna Springer is also the chief psychologist at the Stella Center.

According to Dr. Springer, the publicity that is generated by these trials can, in some instances, motivate survivors to continue speaking out against sexual assault and in support of victims, while in other instances, it can be retraumatizing.

Springer explains, "When survivors of sexual assault report the assault, everything from collecting evidence to sharing their story in public takes so much courage, and when that is not met with justice, or when someone is convicted and then released on a legal technicality, that can promote the message that survivors of assault cannot defend themselves or cannot get justice." "When someone is convicted and then released on a legal technicality, that can promote the message that survivors of assault cannot defend themselves or cannot get justice."

According to Jeglic, "When a high-profile case such as Cosby's is overturned, this raises survivors' feelings of helplessness and hopelessness to the forefront and might retrigger the trauma."

According to Jeglic, the news can also cause physiological reactions among those who have survived. It can make the brain react as if it were back in a traumatic situation, which can trigger a fight-or-flight response and cause symptoms like shortness of breath, racing heart, nausea, trouble focusing, feelings of panic, and depersonalization or derealization, which is the feeling of being disconnected from your surroundings or as if you are having an out-of-body experience.

If you or someone you care about is feeling shocked or retraumatized by the news that Bill Cosby was released from prison and other stories along those lines, the first step is to acknowledge the unfairness. When dealing with challenging feelings, it is crucial to recognize that such feelings are valid.

However, it is helpful to have a stockpile of coping skills that you can turn to in the event that you find yourself being overrun by these ideas and sensations.

CHAPTER ONE

SEXUAL ABUSE AND ASSAULTS TYPES

Any form of sexual violence, including rape, child molestation, incest, and similar forms of sexual contact that is not consented to by the victim, is considered to be sexual abuse. The majority of experts on sexual abuse are of the opinion that sexual abuse is never simply about sex. Instead, it is frequently an attempt to assert one's dominance over other people.

After a sexual attack, getting help in a crisis situation as soon as possible can be extremely beneficial and even save lives. Calling the local police to report an assault of a sexual nature is an option. A medical checkup in a hospital can be something else that survivors want to do.

Individuals who have a history of sexual abuse may find benefit from participating in psychotherapy. There are therapists who focus their practice on helping clients recover from the trauma of sexual assault. Some people who have been sexually abused may do better with help over a longer time period.

THE VARIOUS FORMS OF SEXUAL ABUSE AND ASSAULT

Abuse of a sexual nature occurs frequently, particularly against women and girls. Women are the victims of 90% of all sexual violence incidents.One in every six women in the United States has been the victim of sexual assault. Abuse of the sexual kind occurs in childhood for one out of every 20 boys and one in every five girls.

Abuse and assault of a sexual nature are both umbrella phrases that can apply to several different types of criminal behavior. These illegal acts include:

Raping someone is sexually assaulting them against their will or against their ability to consent. A person is guilty of rape if they are made to have sexual contact against their will while they are under the influence of alcohol or drugs, or if they are not of legal age to give their consent. A date rape is a sexual assault that takes place between two people who already have a romantic or intimate relationship. Only a few states restrict their definition of rape to include only instances of forced sexual encounters. However, any sort of coercive sexual contact with another person might have long-term consequences for that individual. The majority of states have moved to classify forced oral sex and other forms of assault that are similar to rape.

Molestation of children: Molestation of children refers to any form of sexual interaction with a youngster. Many of the children who are sexually abused are too young to understand what is going on, and they are not likely to fight back. In circumstances like these, some people who abused the child will use the youngster's cooperation as "proof" that no one was hurt. Molestation of a child is when someone touches or asks a child to do something sexual without the parent's permission.

Incest is a term that refers to sexual intercourse that takes place between family members who are connected too closely to be married to one another. Incestuous sexual behavior between two adults who are both consenting to it is possible, but it is not very common. The majority of cases of reported incest involve some form of child maltreatment. According to the most recent statistics, more than a third of sexual assault survivors in the United States who are under the age of 18 have been molested by a family member. On the other hand, because incest is a crime that is rarely reported, the number of people who have survived incest may be significantly larger.

Any unwelcome sexual touching, such as grabbing or pinching, is considered to be an example of non-consensual sexual contact and falls under this category. In some cases, this category may also include an attempted rape.

Abuse that does not involve physical contact with the victim is one form of sexual assault that does not cleanly fit into traditional psychological or legal classifications. For instance, sexual abuse occurs when a parent has sex in front of their child or when a parent makes comments to their child that are sexually improper. Another sort of sexual assault is that which is known as "revenge pornography," which refers to websites that distribute naked pictures of people without their permission.

The rules that govern sexual abuse are continuously subject to revision. When it comes to establishing whether or not a person has been the victim of sexual assault, the majority of the specialists who work with survivors of sexual abuse rely on the person's feelings rather than the law. For instance, marital rape can be a very traumatic experience, especially when it occurs in a relationship that is generally abusive. However, the act of raping a spouse did not become illegal anywhere until the 1970s.To this day, it is a crime that is difficult to prosecute.

THE ISSUE OF SEXUAL ASSAULT IN THE ARMY

There is a significant incidence of sexual assault in the armed forces of the United States. According to a report from the year 2014:

A little less than 5% of all women serving in active duty and 1% of all men serving in active duty have said they were sexually touched without their permission.

Penetrative sexual assault accounted for over half of all incidents reported by female victims (rape or penetration with an object). Men experienced this rate at a rate of 35%.

Because of the disparity in the number of women and men serving in the armed forces, men are more likely to be victims of sexual assault. When compared to civilian men, the risk of sexual assault for a guy serving in the armed forces is ten times higher.

The majority of those responsible for these acts are driven by a desire to assert their dominance. Offenders frequently have the desire to exert control over others they view as "inferior." Rarely, is sexual attraction the driving force behind something.

While conversing with someone who cannot be seen, a man in a uniform fidgets with his hands.

There is a problem with reporting sexual assaults that occur among service members. According to studies, barely one in every four people who survive sexual assault in the military will report their experiences. An estimated 81 percent of male survivors of sexual assault never tell anyone.

People who report their assaults are frequently subjected to reprisals from their attackers. In 2014, 62 percent of female reporters reported facing retaliation for their work.Colleagues turned their backs on several of them or blamed them for the attack. Survivors of sexual assault, regardless of gender, may experience repercussions in their professional careers. Some of them have even been discharged from the armed forces.

There may be obstacles for reporters to accessing mental health therapy as well. According to research, the military may have given a number of individuals who reported sexual assault a fake diagnosis of personality disturbances as a pretext to discharge them. Personality disturbances are considered to be a pre-existing disorder by the Department of Veterans Affairs. As a result, it only sometimes pays for the cost of mental health care for survivors.

MALE VICTIMS OF SEXUAL ASSAULT AND ABUSE

Men who have been the victims of sexual assault can endure a significant amount of stigma. The idea that males always want sex is actively encouraged by American culture. There is a widespread misconception that men cannot potentially be victims of rape.

When men disclose being the victims of sexual assault, they are frequently met with skepticism and scorn. Some people might blame the man's "weakness" or his purported homosexuality for the abusive treatment he received. When a guy accuses a woman of sexual misconduct, there is an increased likelihood that the victim will be blamed.

Male survivors may be reluctant to identify their experiences as rape or abuse because of the stigma associated with such terms. It's possible that some people won't bring up the incident at all. On the other hand, men's unwillingness to reveal the condition can impede them from receiving therapy. To get through traumatic experiences, some men turn to harmful coping mechanisms such as substance misuse or cutting themselves.

Assault and Abuse of a Sexual Nature Within the LGBTQ+ Community

The rates of sexual assault for those who identify as homosexual or bisexual are either equivalent to or greater than the rates for individuals who identify as straight. Many sexual assaults committed against LGBTQ+ people are motivated by bias or hatred.

The following is a list of the lifetime prevalence rates for rape among cisgender women:

- Women who identify as bisexual account for 46% of the total.
- Lesbians account for 13% of all females.
- For women who identify as heterosexual, the figure is 17%.
- Statistics on rapes committed by men who identify as cisgender are few. Here is a list of the lifetime prevalence rates for different types of sexual assaults, excluding rape:

- For bisexual men, the figure is 47%.
- 40% of the gay men in the sample.
- Only 21% of men identify as straight.

It is estimated that roughly 64% of transgender people will be sexually assaulted at some point in their lives.This figure includes people who identify as transgender regardless of their sexual orientation or gender identity. Transgender children and young adults are at an increased risk for sexual assault. In 2011, a poll asked transgender students, "Have you ever been sexually attacked at school by a peer or member of staff?" One-twelfth of them said "yes."

The figure is shown in silhouette carrying a rainbow umbrella as they look out over an empty field.

It is common for sexual assaults to go unreported within the LGBTQ+ community. There is a possibility that survivors will be afraid to disclose their sexual orientation or gender identity to others. It's possible that they don't believe the judicial system will protect them. There is also the possibility that survivors will incite additional violence.

People who identify as LGBTQ+ frequently face stigmatization after reporting sexual assault, just like other survivors. There is a possibility that survivors will be denied care due to discrimination in the healthcare system. It's possible that close friends and relatives will believe the negative preconceptions about LGBTQ+ people and place the blame on the victim. It is possible for members of the LGBTQ+ community in a certain area to not believe the victim of domestic violence or to not hold the abuser accountable when it happens.

A therapist is available to assist LGBTQ+ people and those who have survived sexual assault. Mental health providers are prohibited from sharing an individual's private information with third parties. In therapy, one can seek support without fear of being judged, which makes it a safe and private environment.

THE RELATIONSHIP BETWEEN RACE/ETHNICITY AND SEXUAL ASSAULT

Certain racial and ethnic groups in the United States are more likely to be victims of sexual assault than others. From the National Intimate Partner and Sexual Violence Survey (NISVS), here is a list of the lifetime prevalence rates for rape:

- 9.5% of women who identify as Asian or Pacific Islanders are unemployed.
- Latinas who are Hispanic account for 15.0 percent of the total.
- White women account for 19.9% of the population.
- Approximately 21% of black females
- Native American women who are American Indian or Alaska Native account for 28.9 percent of the total.
- For multiracial women, the figure is 31.8 percent.

The paper in question did not include data on male survivors.

Racism puts people of other races and ethnicities at a higher risk of sexual assault.There is a widespread fetishization of people of color as "exotic" and hypersexual beings. As a consequence of this, survivors have a greater chance of being classified as "voluntary" participants. When sexual assaults are committed against white people, the penalties are usually harsher than when they are committed against people of color.

As a consequence of this, people of color are significantly less likely to disclose having been the victims of sexual assault. There are certain people who do not have faith that they will be treated properly by the judicial system. When others disclose personal information, they can worry that they are "betraying" their community. There are various instances in which cultural norms contribute to the additional stigma that people who report facing These factors may also discourage survivors from getting treatment for their mental health issues.

ABUSE OF CHILDREN IN THE CONTEXT OF SEX

Abuse of minors on a sexual level can take many different forms. It could be a complete stranger, or it could be someone as close as a parent. For a child to be subjected to sexual abuse, physical contact is not required. Voyeuristic behaviors, which include watching a youngster shower or undress, are considered a kind of sexual abuse. Adults who harm children by exposing their genitalia to minors are also guilty of child abuse.

It's possible that an adult who sexually exploits minors also has a sexual interest in the young people they exploit. However, sexual attraction is not a prerequisite for engaging in abusive behavior. Abusing a child is often done so that the abuser can gain power over the child.

Sexual assaults on children are all too common. This also applies to the United States:

44 percent of those who have been sexually assaulted are under the age of 18.

When they are between the ages of 7 and 13, children are most susceptible to being sexually assaulted.

Ten percent of children in the United States are abused before the age of 18.

Twenty percent of sexually abused children have their first sexual experience before the age of eight.

Children who have been abused do not always immediately report it, despite the fact that it is extremely common. This could be attributed, in part, to the offender's control over the youngster in question.

Up to 93% of children who have been sexually abused are intimately familiar with the person who molested them. The abuser will often use threats or other ways to control the child to keep the child from telling anyone about the abuse.

More than a third of those who abuse children are related to the victim in some way.

Seventy-three percent of abused children fail to report the incident for at least a year.

At least 45 percent of abused children do not come forward for at least five years after the incident.

Despite the fact that it can be challenging to identify sexual abuse in young people, detection is still feasible. If a youngster demonstrates any of the following potential red flags, there may be reason for concern:

Underwear that is torn or soiled

Infections of the urinary tract or yeast can occur frequently.

Apprehension and bad dreams right before bedtime

Bedwetting after the normal age is considered normal.

Concerned with the appearance of their physique,

Anger and tantrums

Disposition that is depressed and withdrawn.

Sexual experience or activities that are not proper for one's age group

The aforementioned indicators are not always conclusive proof that a child is a victim of sexual abuse. It's possible that children are acting this way because of another problem. However, proof is not required in order to report an incident of child abuse. The mission of Child Protective Services (CPS) is to gather evidence. To file a report of abuse, one needs only to have a "reasonable suspicion" that it is occurring in order to do so.

Disclosure of sexual abuse to authorities may protect a youngster from developing mental health problems later in life. Those who were victims of sexual abuse as children have a much increased likelihood of developing substance use disorders or concerns related to food and eating. They also have an increased risk of experiencing sexual abuse as adults.

You are free to contact the child protective services of your state if you have any reason to believe that a child is being harmed in any way.

WHAT EXACTLY IS INTENTIONAL SEXUAL HARASSMENT?

The term "sexual assault" is frequently used interchangeably with the term "sexual harassment." Even though both sexual assault and sexual harassment involve sexual contact that was not started by the victim, there are major differences between the two.

The phrase "sexual harassment" is frequently used in the context of legal proceedings. The Equal Employment Opportunity Commission of the United States says that the following actions are sexual harassment:

Unwanted sexual advances or contact might be seen as harassment.

The harassment of a person based on their sexual orientation or identity

Making sexist jokes or comments regarding a specific sexual orientation is insulting.

There was a lot of pressure to go on dates or perform sexual favors for other people.

Sexual harassment can take place in any setting. However, the majority of the laws that protect individuals who may be subjected to such behavior focus on the prevention of such behavior in the workplace. Sexual harassment includes things like making sexual comments or gestures, staring, calling someone names like "babe" or "hunk," and giving unwanted or personal gifts.

PROBLEMS WITH MENTAL HEALTH THAT ARE THE RESULT OF SEXUAL ABUSE

Survivors of sexual assault may experience feelings that their bodies are not truly their own after the assault. Survivors frequently describe a range of emotions, including shame, dread, and remorse. A lot of people blame themselves for the attack.

Survivors of sexual abuse may be at increased risk for mental health disorders as a result of the traumatic experiences and unpleasant feelings associated with the abuse. Those who survive sexual abuse run the risk of developing:

Depression can make it difficult to come to terms with the loss of control over one's own body. It has the potential to bring on feelings of helplessness and despair. It is also possible for one's feeling of self-worth to diminish as a result of it. Depression can be mild and short-lived, or it can be severe and last for a long time.

Extreme anxiety can be brought on by a lack of control over one's physical functions. Those who survived the assault might be concerned that it could occur once more. It's possible that some people will have panic attacks. Others could acquire a fear of open spaces, known as agoraphobia, and become unable to leave their houses. A survivor may, in some instances, grow to have an ongoing irrational dread of the kind of person who caused them damage. If a tall, blond, blue-eyed man sexually assaulted someone, that person may have a natural dislike, suspicion, or fear of all men who fit that description.

A survivor of sexual assault may develop posttraumatic stress disorder (PTSD), which is characterized by strong memories of the violence suffered. Sometimes the disruption caused by flashbacks is so severe that it causes a survivor to become disoriented and forget where they are. Complex posttraumatic stress, a related condition, can also develop in a person who has experienced traumatic events (C-PTSD). In addition to the symptoms of classic PTSD, people who suffer from C-PTSD also experience a persistent fear of being abandoned. People who suffer from C-PTSD may also have disruptions in their personalities.

Disturbances of personality: Sexual abuse can occasionally lead to personality disruptions like borderline personality. It's possible that the conduct associated with personality changes is simply an adaptation to the abuse. A dread of being alone is one example of a trait associated with people who have a borderline personality. It's possible that this dread won't serve you well as an adult. On the other hand, a person who was never abandoned as a child might have been spared the trauma of sexual assault.

Attachment problems might arise for survivors, making it difficult for them to build healthy ties with other people. This is especially true for children who have been subjected to physical or sexual abuse. Those who experienced childhood abuse as children are more likely to develop attachment issues as adults. It's possible that they have trouble getting close to people or are too eager to do so.

Addiction: According to the findings of certain studies, those who have survived abuse are 26 times more likely to take drugs. Substance misuse and alcoholism are two ways to dull the agony of being abused. But drug abuse often leads to a number of problems.

Scars of a psychological kind are not the only ones left by sexual abuse. It is also possible for this to have long-term effects on one's health.

A person who is abused could end up with scrapes and cuts on their body. They may also have suffered more serious wounds, such as cuts with a knife, broken bones, or damage to their genitalia. Some people experience persistent pain without any visible underlying physical condition.

Some survivors experience sexual dysfunction and difficulties with fertility. Others run the risk of contracting sexually transmitted diseases. It is a common misconception that sexual assault cannot result in pregnancy, but in reality, this is not always the case. In situations where a youngster becomes pregnant, the act of giving birth could pose serious health risks to the child.

ADVICE AND COUNSELING AFTER INTIMATE PARTNER VIOLENCE AND ABUSE

A significant number of people end up with mental health disorders after surviving a sexual attack. You are not "weak" or "broken" simply because you are struggling with your mental health. There is no one right way to recover from a traumatic experience.

A mental health professional is someone who can provide assistance to people who have endured sexual assault. Counseling provides a secure, confidential environment in which one can seek assistance without fear of being judged. You do not have to figure out solutions to your difficulties on your own.

CHAPTER TWO

PSYCHOLOGICAL IMPACTS

The psychological aftermath of being sexually assaulted might seem very different for different people. A youngster who is the victim of sexual assault could be unaware of it for years. A victim of rape who is an adult may try to convince themselves that the act was voluntary, especially if it occurred during a date.

A person who has been assaulted by a stranger is likely to be filled with a great deal of terror. If someone was attacked by someone they knew, they may still have trouble trusting other people.

It does not matter how you are feeling now. There is no predetermined timetable for when you should start to feel better. Everyone's experience is unique.

However, it is not uncommon to have feelings of embarrassment, bewilderment, and guilt. A survivor may have regrets about their inability to halt the assault. It's possible that they're concerned about what other people will think of them, or that they might blame themselves (despite the fact that it's never the victim's responsibility).

The vast majority of people who survived say that they have flashbacks, which are mental replays of the attack.

Sexual assault survivors may also be more likely to have problems with their mental health, such as the following:

Depression

PTSD

Substance use disorders

Eating disorders

Anxiety

Those who have experienced multiple assaults may be at an even greater risk for mental health concerns than those who have just experienced one.

And unfavorable comments from friends, family members, or professionals may even further raise the chance of having issues with one's mental health. Greater psychological trauma is caused when a person is not believed (or when they are blamed).

Help from the professionals

A mental health professional is someone who can help you deal with the effects of a sexual assault, whether it happened a long time ago or just yesterday.

Working through difficulties in a setting that is safe, private, and free from judgment is one of the goals of therapy. Your therapist might be able to help you work through your feelings, find new ways to deal with problems, and learn how to handle stress better.

You are able to talk about particular topics, such as how to cope with flashbacks or how to get a better night's sleep. You should also think about whether or not you want to disclose the fact that you were assaulted to your close friends or members of your family.

There are numerous approaches to dealing with the aftermath of sexual assault. The following are some examples of common therapies:

In cognitive behavioral therapy, therapists may aid clients in detecting and replacing the beliefs and behaviors that contribute to their misery. This is an important step in the treatment process.

EMDR stands for eye movement desensitization and reprocessing, and it's an interactive therapy that's used to treat traumatic experiences and cut down on distress. While discussing a traumatic experience, it's common for people to tap their fingers or move their eyes back and forth.

In supportive therapy, therapists may assist clients in making sense of their feelings and determining the tools that they can use to manage their symptoms.

If you suffer from a certain mental health condition, such as anxiety or depression, medication may be an option to help alleviate the symptoms. You should talk to both your primary care doctor and your therapist about this to figure out if it's right for you.

There is also the possibility of taking part in group therapy. Your therapist could suggest that you join a support group for a particular condition, such as acquiring the skills necessary to cope with traumatic experiences. However, because group therapy isn't appropriate for everyone, you should consider this option with the professional who is treating you.

There is also the possibility of joining a support group. In support groups, people who have been sexually assaulted can talk to other people who have been through the same thing.

Methods of Handling Difficulty

Experts in mental health may be able to help you figure out what changes to your lifestyle and ways to deal with stress will help you the most.

Abilities to relax your body and mind. There are a variety of coping tactics that can help calm your body's physiological responses, such as yoga and progressive muscle relaxation, and you can choose whichever one you enjoy the most (like a rapid heartbeat).

Ways to confront your anxieties and overcome them. A significant number of people who have survived sexual assault will go to considerable lengths to ensure they are not brought back to the experience. Your therapist can assist you in identifying and developing coping mechanisms that will make it easier for you to confront it. This has the potential to be an important part of moving forward.

Having the ability to control your thoughts. A sexual assault may have a variety of effects on your day-to-day thinking, including intrusive thoughts, flashbacks, and catastrophic predictions, to name just a few. A therapist may be able to assist you in developing coping mechanisms to put an end to these ideas or to handle them in such a way that they do not have a negative impact on your mental health.

Your therapist will work with you to figure out the best ways to help you deal with your symptoms.

They can also help you avoid turning to unhealthy coping mechanisms like alcohol and drugs, which may be what you're tempted to do in times of stress.

The experience of being the victim of sexual assault is one that is quite terrible. Nevertheless, it doesn't have to be the end of your existence. A significant number of survivors find healthy ways to move on with their lives and recover from the horrific event.

If you are unsure where to look for assistance, talk to your primary care physician or get in touch with a mental health expert in your area. There's also the possibility of therapy being done online.

It is not a sign of weakness to seek assistance from others. Reaching out to others is an act that requires a lot of strength and bravery. However, doing so can assist you in recovering from the trauma linked to the sexual attack you experienced.

CHAPTER THREE

THE MANAGEMENT STRATEGIES

Cut off totally from the news and social media.

Research has shown that providing sexual assault survivors with ongoing reminders of situations similar to their previous experiences is more likely to cause them harm than to assist them. She explains that even though you might be interested in learning more about what took place, being constantly exposed to the specifics of the crimes and the reactions of others can actually make the trauma symptoms worse.

Rely on the people and resources that are there for you.

According to Springer, having people in your life who are supportive of you is essential to healing if you are a survivor of sexual assault. Springer goes on to say that having a support system can help survivors if they feel activated or retraumatized by Cosby's being freed or other scenarios that are similar.

"If a survivor has people in their corner who believe them, who have been down this road before, or who have advocated for them, in other words, a 'tribe' of people that support them, they are going to be protected from some of the negative effects of what they can't control," Springer explains. "If a survivor has people in their corner who believe them, who have been down this road before, or who have advocated for them, in other words, a community

I am of the same opinion, and suggest that you give a close friend, a member of your family, or your therapist a call and let them know that you are having difficulties.

They make use of different grounding techniques.

According to the experts at James Madison University, grounding techniques are activities that are relaxing and help alleviate anxiety and stress by replacing your focus on thoughts of the past with a connection to what is currently happening around you (JMU).

Methods of re-grounding that involve making use of one's senses of sight, smell, taste, hearing, and touch are particularly helpful for people who have survived sexual assault. If you make use of all five of your senses, it will be easier for you to remain rooted in the present and have fewer flashbacks. Per JMU, some strategies include:

Put some weight on the balls of your feet and press firmly into the ground to help you focus on where you are.

Keep a picture that makes you feel calm with you at all times, and when you feel anxious, look at that picture.

Take note of the people, things, and sounds that are in your immediate environment.

Candles with pleasant scents can be lit, or you could go to a place like a bakery or coffee shop that has a pleasant aroma.

Pet or interact with an animal, whether it's your own pet or an animal at a local shelter.Animals thrive on human interaction.

You might find it helpful to listen to a familiar audiobook or album instead.

Dedicate some time each day to the practice of mindfulness meditation.

According to the Cleveland Clinic, mindfulness is a type of meditation that entails focusing on what is happening in the present moment and being aware of any thoughts, sensations, or feelings that you have without judging them.

If you are interested in giving mindfulness a shot, one practice you can try is concentrating on the sensation of your breath as it enters and leaves your body. This can help you stay in the present if you start to think or feel like you are reliving a traumatic event, because it will keep you from going back into the past.

According to the Cleveland Clinic, another way that meditation can help you relax is by slowing your breathing rate and allowing tight muscles to become more relaxed.

Refrain from using illicit substances and from drinking alcohol.

According to the University of Michigan, if you have experienced a traumatic event such as a sexual assault, you may feel the temptation to turn to drugs or alcohol in order to dull your reaction to triggers or distressing memories of your experience. However, doing so can actually make the symptoms of post-traumatic stress disorder (PTSD) worse.

While there is a natural tendency to want to numb the emotional pain, using drugs and alcohol will only make the situation worse. "While there may be a tendency to want to numb the emotional pain,"

It is possible that, in the long run, it will unintentionally contribute to the development of a substance abuse disorder, which occurs when someone engages in compulsive drinking or drug use to the point where it interferes with their ability to carry out daily activities. According to the experts at the

University of Michigan, this could pave the way for relationship problems with loved ones, problems at work, and even health problems.

Seek Assistance in Case You Require It

Talk to a therapist or someone else in the mental health field if you feel like you're being retraumatized or triggered.

These new treatments can really alleviate suffering in a very efficient manner without necessarily requiring survivors to talk through details of their assault, as Springer explains. "There are ways to treat many of the most severe symptoms without having survivors share the worst day of their experience repeatedly," she says. "These new treatments can really alleviate suffering."

It is advisable that you get in touch with the Rape, Abuse, and Incest National Network (RAINN) if you are unsure of how to get started or where to turn for assistance. RAINN is a non-profit organization that provides resources for people who have survived sexual assault or abuse.

CHAPTER FOUR

SPOTTING SEXUAL ABUSE

Abuse of any kind is a terrible thing to go through, but there are ways that you may receive help for yourself if you find yourself in this situation. Talk to someone who cares about you, contact a crisis hotline, or dial 911 if you are in urgent danger. It is possible that you will need to work through a great deal of emotional grief if you are a survivor of abuse. You may want to seek help from counseling and support groups to help you through the process of recovering from sexual abuse, as it may be a frustrating process that takes a long time and can take a long time.

Determine the indicators of abuse in adults. Adults who were sexually molested as children are more likely to display evidence of lasting trauma as adults, which can have an effect on both a person's physical and mental health. Some frequent signs that someone was molested while they were a youngster include the following:

- reacting with fear whenever reminders of the attack are brought up.
- Having a sense of uneasiness and danger
- experiencing disturbing flashbacks of the attack.
- having difficulty concentrating on something.
- Persistent thoughts of wrongdoing, resentment, and/or melancholy
- Having a negative perception of oneself

- Having issues with one's interpersonal connections
- A decline in sexual interest

Be on the lookout for warning indicators of sexual abuse in adolescents. The ways in which teenagers react to being sexually abused are not always dissimilar to one another. Check for the following typical warning indicators in adolescents:

- self-hurting self-(cutting, burning)
- Having inadequate personal hygiene
- misusing substances or alcohol, or both.
- engaging in sexual activity with multiple partners on multiple occasions.
- attempting to get away from home.
- displaying symptoms consistent with depression or anxiety.
- putting forth an effort to commit suicide.
- exhibiting behavior that suggests a fear of proximity or intimacy.

- alterations in appetite, including but not limited to dieting and obsessive eating.

Acquire the knowledge necessary to identify the symptoms of sexual abuse in children. Although children may react to sexual abuse in slightly different ways, there are some common markers that may help you recognize sexual abuse in children. If you look for these indicators, you may be able to spot instances of sexual abuse in children. There are a number of warning indicators, including the following:

- Alterations in the normal routine of sleeping or sleep disruptions such as having nightmares
- Changes in appetite or eating habits have occurred.
- A sudden mood swing
- In your games, your writing, your drawings, or even your conversations, leave signals about abuse.
- becomes anxious or concerned about a particular individual or location.
- He or she discusses a new older buddy and/or refuses to disclose secrets that he or she has with this person while simultaneously doing so.
- For no apparent reason, is given money, presents, or toys by another person.
- Being turned off by oneself or by their own body
- They appear to be adults in terms of their understanding of sexual behavior.

CHAPTER FIVE

GETTING HELP AFTER ABUSE

If your safety is in jeopardy right now, you should call the emergency services. If you are in immediate danger of being abused, go as far away from the person as you can and phone 911 as soon as possible to obtain help. If you are in immediate danger of being abused, get as far away from the person as you can. If you are able to, you should make an effort to leave the house and go to a public location. If this is not possible, you should lock yourself in a room and wait for aid to arrive.

Gain an understanding of what constitutes sexual abuse. Abuse of a sexual nature might occur repeatedly or only once. In either case, it can be challenging to define what constitutes abuse and what does not fall into that category. It may be helpful for you to respond appropriately if you have a better understanding of the behaviors that constitute sexual abuse or assault. For instance, you could be under the assumption that it is impossible for a person's spouse to sexually assault them. However, this is not the case. This belief is not correct, but it does occasionally prevent people from seeking help when they really need it. If you're not sure if you've been sexually abused or not, think about the following questions:

Have you or someone else been the target of unwanted sexual or physical contact from another person who did not have your consent to do so?

Have you ever been forced to have sexual relations with another person in spite of your repeated demands that they desist? This can involve threatening you or making you feel bad about saying no to something you want.

Does someone frequently try to control you, either physically or psychologically, in the ways that you spend time together? This might include purposely making you fearful or guilty about leaving them, or it could entail forcing you to have intimate contact with other people whom you do not wish to have intimate contact with.

Talk it over with a supportive person in your life. Talk to a reliable person, such as a mentor or a loved one, or even a guidance counselor, and explain the problem to them. Sexual predators bank on their victims to keep quiet and keep their secrets hidden, but you may put an end to the cycle by telling someone about what has been occurring to you and by keeping their confidence. Share the news with someone as soon as you can. It has been demonstrated that one of the most useful things for you to do in order to deal with the repercussions of sexual abuse is to construct a solid support system around yourself. This is something that you can accomplish. The following are some suggestions that can help you create and strengthen your support system:

Accept invitations to things, even if the first time you go makes you feel bad and uncomfortable.

Don't hold your breath for an invitation to go anywhere. Just make the first move and give someone a call.

Participate in activities on campus and in the surrounding community, like events hosted in resident halls or on campus, or get-togethers with your family.

Engage in chat with the individual sitting next to you in the classroom or at the community event you're attending. It's possible that you're introducing yourself to a new friend right now.

Discuss topics that could be of interest to other people. Be an observant listener.

Dial the number listed for assistance. If you feel uncomfortable talking to someone you know about the sexual abuse you have experienced, you can get help by calling a sexual abuse hotline. They may be able to provide you with information on local resources in your town, such as centers for victims of domestic abuse, where you can go to obtain individual help. The following are some examples of hotlines that you can call:

(608) 392-7804 or (800) 362-5454, ext. 7804.The services provided by Safe Path are both strictly confidential and at no cost.

RAINN's National Sexual Assault Hotline offers the following services: Dial 1-800-656-HOPE to be connected to the rape crisis center that is most conveniently located for you (4673).

1-877-739-3895 is the number to call for the National Sexual Violence Resource Center (NSVRC).

CHAPTER SIX

DEALING WITH THE EMOTIONAL PAIN

Think about seeing a therapist or counselor. You may still be feeling lingering physiological repercussions of the trauma caused by the abuse, even if you are no longer being abused or assaulted, even if the violence has stopped. This kind of trauma is quite similar to PTSD. Your everyday life may suddenly present you with unexpected instances of great anxiety and terror, as well as flashbacks from the traumatic experience. A lot of the time, the wounds stay even after years have passed since the abuse has stopped, and a lot of people seek the support of counselors in order to get more assistance in overcoming the effects of their past.

A mental health counselor or therapist can give you a supportive ear and numerous ways to help you overcome the effects of any trauma that you may be holding on to. They can also help you determine whether or not you are holding on to any trauma at all.

Counseling services are frequently provided by groups that deal with domestic violence to victims of that type of violence as well as victims of sexual assault.

Understand that this is not your fault. Realizing that it is not your fault that you are or were being sexually abused is one of the most crucial steps in recognizing and leaving the clutches of sexual abuse. This is one of the most important steps in escaping the clutches of sexual abuse. It is essential that you do not allow feelings of guilt or shame to prevent you from telling others about your experience or from seeking assistance for yourself. Guilt or shame may surface as a result of the actions of the perpetrator or as a result of the way in which you are treated by people you tell. It is essential that you understand that it is never your fault if another person assaults or abuses you in any way.

People who mistreat others do so because they choose to. They made the decision to take advantage of you despite the fact that you may have been vulnerable or foolish.

Abusers are capable of playing mental games. They could be able to persuade you of things that are not true, and they might lead you to believe that you are not deserving of love and care.

Exhibit some kindness toward yourself. It is possible that it will be some time before you feel back to normal after being the victim of an assault or persistent abuse. It is crucial that you do not take out your frustration on yourself during this time because you may feel frustrated and it is important that you do not take out your displeasure on yourself. Recognize that in order to heal fully, it will take some time and that the process will be difficult for you.

Imagine that a close friend was going through what you are going through right now. Consider how long it would take them to get better and what you would say to them at that point in time. Make an effort to apply this level of empathy to yourself.

Allow yourself some time to cry and be upset with yourself. Because of the terrible occurrence that happened to you, you will, of course, have a tough time processing your feelings about it. Let yourself be upset. Give yourself permission to feel everything from rage to sadness to confusion and everything in between. This is a natural and expected step in the recovery process.

Spend time with the people that mean the most to you. Find the people in your life who are the most important to you, the ones who can cheer you up and help you feel more relaxed, and focus on cultivating those relationships. Spend some time with them by calling them on the phone or going to the kitchen with them. You will recover more quickly with the assistance of others around you.

Describe in writing what you are thinking and how you are feeling. Writing about your experiences is a good way to start expressing your anger and resentment over the things that have happened to you. You should begin writing in a journal on a daily basis, even if it's just a few sentences. Write about anything that comes to mind at the moment. Some people find that it helps them to talk about the abuse they have been through.

Make contact with other people who have experienced the same kind of abuse. You are going to need to continue communicating with individuals who care about you and who understand you while you get well. Participating in a support group for those who have survived sexual assault is a great way to connect with others who can empathize with what you are going through. These support groups can provide a secure environment for you to talk about your experience and listen to what other people have gone through, which may help you realize that you are not the only one going through what you are.

Take action to reclaim control of the situation. It is not uncommon to struggle with decision-making or to have feelings that you are not in control of the situation you find yourself in. Beginning to make choices regarding your treatment and your life going forward is the single most effective step you can take to reclaim some measure of control over your life. Collect as much information as you can about the circumstances you find yourself in, then decide how you want to react to what you've learned.

You should seek the assistance of a lawyer if you intend to press charges for rape or domestic abuse. They will guide you through the legal proceedings.

Find a doctor who can help you find care for any injuries or diseases you might have.

Find a counselor who can assist you in working through the issue so that you can heal emotionally.

www.ingramcontent.com/pod-product-compliance
Lightning Source LLC
LaVergne TN
LVHW052107160826
845678LV00015B/3405

* 9 7 9 8 8 4 4 1 7 3 7 5 2 *